By Gary Beck

Novels

Extreme Change
Acts of Defiance
Flawed Connections
Call to Valor
Sudden Conflicts
Wave Length

Crumbling Ramparts
Flare Up
Raise High the Walls
Still Defiant
State of Rage

Poetry

Expectations
Days of Destruction
Dawn in Cities
Assault on Nature
Songs of a Clerk
Civilized Ways
Conditioned Response
Displays
Resonance
Perceptions
Fault Lines
Tremors
Virtual Living
Perturbations

Blossoms of Decay
Rude Awakenings
Blunt Force
The Remission of Order
Contusions
Transitions
Earth Links
Mortal Coil
Desperate Seeker
Too Harsh For Pastels
Temporal Dreams
Severance
Redemption Value
Fractional Disorder

Play Collections

The Big Match and other one act plays
Collected Plays of Gary Beck Volume I
Plays of Aristophanes translated then directed by Gary Beck

Short Story Collections

A Glimpse of Youth
Now I Accuse and other stories
Dogs Don't Send Flowers and other stories

Essays

Collected Essays of Gary Beck

Disruptions

Gary Beck

Contents

To Arla, who suffers one disruption after another, but keeps her
determination and good spirits.

Confined

I sit in prison cell
still revolted by the smell
of fellow inmates,
some more animal than human
after years in cages
barely ventilated,
insufficiently cleaned,
storehouse of bodily waste,
and the snores, belches, farts,
a surreal symphony
of primordial sounds
that keep me up at night
when my fatigued body
clamors for restful sleep.
But I think of the inmates,
most guilty of a crime
trying to endure the time
with many years to go
before they are set free
in an alien land
that will not welcome
the men who are unfit
to join the evolved world.

Ousted

I saw a vireo in Bryant Park
who was suffering
Post Traumatic Meadow Syndrome,
too confused to eat breadcrumbs
having been summarily evicted
by encroaching agri-business
to grow marketable crops,
sending avian denizens to the cities,
just like people come to the cities
when there homes are taken
by eminent domain.

Progress

I look forward
to the driverless car
that will eliminate
drunken driving,
carjacking,
tailgating,
leaving the scene of an accident,
all the other abuses
inflicted by human drivers
on our fellow citizens.

Maximum Resistance

When prey are grabbed by predators
in the animal kingdom
a tranquilizing submission
takes possession of the soul
of the helpless victim
making death less painful.

Humans lived the same way
for thousands of years,
resigned to their condition
blindly accepting fate,
most bound to the land
in the service of a master
who determined existence.

There were always exceptions,
men who were more than animals,
but there probably weren't many,
or they would have been destroyed
the early stages of cooperation
and we never would have evolved
beyond the tribal system.

But another breed arose
rejecting brutish conditions
and united, and built cities,
created a new environment
that superficially resembled
the traditional way of life,

yet fostered greater isolation,
despite proximity.

And a middle class emerged
who asserted their beliefs
that they were as good
as anyone else.
And the owners of the land
tolerated them for a while,
until they began to imagine
that they governed the land.

Then the owners of the land
began the deaccession
of those who had forgotten
who the rulers were.
All their art collections,
luxurious houses,
the material things
that comforted their lives
were slowly taken away
and they no longer possessed
narcotic acceptance
to ease remaining days.

Removed

I visited a foreign land
and took long walks on the beach
where the privileged safely basked
shaded from the burning sun
by large, colorful umbrellas,
guarded by alert protectors
ignoring sensual bodies
weighed down by jewels and tablets,
completely enrapt in shopping
for goods denied the masses,
while the men babble business deals
intent on making more money
to acquire more costly treasure.

E Pluribus Unum

Once we built a country
made it run,
worked on it all the time,
brought in lots of strangers
made them one,
now its become a crime.
Separate this. Separate that.
The myth of unity
fraying beyond repair,
as different agendas
are more important
then the fate of the nation
and we finally resemble
the old world.

Battered America

Our people are beleaguered
feeling trapped, desperate,
so they turn to the unfit
accepting false promises
for better times, more jobs,
and elect diminutive leaders
incapable of problem solving,
only making things worse
by denying climate change
despite unprecedented storms,
droughts, wild fires
devastating our nation,
while the president plays golf,
assailing those who disagree with him,
vindictively pursuing those who oppose him,
refusing to learn how to lead a nation,
instead insulting his predecessors
criticizing everything before he took office,
dismembering the agencies of progress,
protecting the interests of the rich,
ignoring the suffering of the poor,
happily going his way
undermining tomorrow.

Hurricane

The wind blew,
the rain fell,
the ocean surged,
until fragile communities
were in danger
of being blown or washed away.
Frightened or sensible people
began to evacuate,
hoping to reach higher ground,
leaving behind possessions
suddenly less valued
by the threatening storm.

Park Dirge

Yesterday I fed two catbirds
in Bryant Park,
a lovely vest pocket venue
with wonderful amenities
for locals and tourists,
not too kind to birds,
except pigeons and sparrows,
hardier then other birds
dwelling in cities.
Yet we do not know
how many perish
in this lovely park
in the battle for survival,
since we never see their bodies,
while people are playing chess,
practicing yoga, eating outdoors,
enjoying the diversions
that conceal the life and death struggle
of birds that cannot compete
with more aggressive birds,
dooming the catbirds,
too urbanized to migrate.

Remnants

The once proud avenues
of vaunted shops
now are deserted.
Only the ghosts
of employees past
haunt the cobwebbed stores,
all that remains of the departed
unable to get other jobs,
abandoned by their masters,
unable to adapt
to changing circumstances,
conditioned to servitude,
unfit for opportunities
limited to the few
capable of functioning
in the Information Age.

Progress II

I think of all the people
killed in automobile accidents,
can only guess at the numbers
millions in America…
How many in the rest of the world?
Drunk drivers, careless drivers,
speeders, lane changers,
and the idiots
on cell phones, texting,
the various disturbances
that prevent control of powerful machines
that have no intelligence
and cannot tell the difference
between responsible drivers
and the many death givers.
I think of all the people
who will oppose driverless cars,
opting instead for murder and mayhem.

Quick Pics

A baseball player
wanting to win
stands for the National Anthem
hand on heart,
but not really listening
intent on getting a hit.

A concentration camp guard
wanting obedience
listens to a Beethoven sonata,
swept away by its beauty,
while his prisoners,
live in terror.

A business man
wanting greater profits
listens to classic rock on his IPOD
while signing the contract
that will move his factory
to another land,
costing thousands of jobs at home.

A politician
wanting more power
listens to whale music,
trying to sooth his seething mind
while plotting and scheming
for higher office,
at the expense of the people.

An immigrant
wanting a better life
listens to salsa,
while trying to quell her fears
that an irate president
frothing about dreamers,
will send her home.

Indifferent Eviction

When I was young
I walked unblemished Florida shores
and saw flights of pelicans
50-100 strong,
going about their business
in orderly vees.
Large flocks of sandpipers
scurried along water's edge
in complete unison,
feeding in rhythmic pecks,
suddenly taking flight
in organized formation
the military would envy.
Few of us notice
the departure of our neighbors
from proximity
to man-made nests,
inhabitants too territorial
to allow coexistence.

Treatment Center

I sit in hospital waiting room.
No one looks happy.
Then I remember
this is a senior facility,
not an emergency room,
which explains
why they look resigned
rather then terrified.
These are not the wealthy
so the services they expect
are minimal,
merely sufficient
to delay conclusion
until the last visit.

City View

Winter in the city
a different picture
without greenery.
Everything is greyer.
After a while
even people are greyer.
Cold winds blow.
Heavy clothes are worn.
The pace is more urgent.
Then it snows.
For a short while
an ermine coat covers
a suddenly elegant cityscape.
But all too quickly
urban soot, emissions
darken the snow,
filthying the streets
no longer lovely
to look at.

The Shattered Calm

A peaceful day in New York City,
bastion of safety in the troubled world.
Tourists explore enticing shops.
Bicyclists take advantage
Of a warm day for a ride.
Pedestrians go for a stroll
delighted to be outside
before the advent of winter.
Suddenly a truck
careens down the street
running down people.
Screams of pain resound,
cries of the terrified
not drowned out
by the roaring engine,
more and more struck
until the truck crashes.
The driver leaps out,
yells 'Allah akbar',
is shot down
by responding police,
but not until too many
are killed or wounded
in what politicians call
'a cowardly attack',
refusing to acknowledge
the West is engaged
in a clash of civilizations.

Hurricane II

A weather front develops
somewhere in the Caribbean.
It grows and gets a category.
A name. Jennifer.
Meteorologists,
armored with PHDs,
tell us the wind is increasing.
Jennifer becomes category 3.
Now she is taken seriously.

Her projected course is charted.
Early warnings go out.
The nuts who fly into storms
take to the air.
News stations forget other items
when category 4 is announced
and the Governor of Florida
orders mass evacuations.

150 miles per hour winds
ravage Caribbean islands,,
but they don't get much attention
since they aren't American islands.
Jennifer grows stronger,
winds 180 to 200 mph.

The state police and National Guard
supervise evacuation
of mid-Florida,

where Jennifer is aiming.
The rain begins to fall,
harder and harder
and the ocean is surging.

The highways are jammed one way,
north, traffic is inching along,
road rage incidents erupt
when one car moves slightly faster.
Engines overheat, cars stall,
drivers pull over,
marooned on the side of the road.
Escape is uncertain.

Some long term residents
refuse to depart
despite rising flood waters,
stubborn citizens
not wanting to leave homes,
prized possessions.
Some are predators
waiting to man their boats,
sail to deserted wealthy houses
abandoned in the flight to safety,
leaving jewels, cash, furs, electronics,
other valuables to be looted,
as long as the authorities
are busy elsewhere
saving lives.

Kinship

The cities in the Western World
have cancerous slums
that consume millions,
but are far removed
from wealthy neighborhoods,
business districts,
shopping centers,
entertainment areas,
creating an illusion
that poverty doesn't exist.

The cities in the Eastern world
have pandemic slums
that consume tens of millions,
and spill their denizens,
poor, ragged, hungry, diseased
into wealthy neighborhoods
business districts,
shopping centers,
entertainment areas
shattering the illusion
that poverty doesn't exist.

Conflicts

Armies march across the globe
subduing peoples.
Rebel groups loot and burn
destroying villages.
Religious movements clash
proclaiming the will of god.
Western democracies
consider themselves
better than others,
yet they all have
poverty populations,
criminal elements,
and abusers of the law,
while only the wealthy
have recourse
to favorable outcomes.

Want Ads

The most dangerous action
of irresponsible scientists
is sending unmanned vehicles
on long voyages
announcing to the universe
where we are.
Please come visit.
It's intelligent to look and listen
to who's out there, somewhere,
so we might know in advance
if they suddenly drop in
for cultural exchanges.
After all, if we can't go to them,
they're obviously more advanced,
so why send them messages
describing how primitive we are,
a gilt invitation
with no requirements
to come in peace,
just like we've always done
when going to new places.
It's too late to withdraw
the public service announcement
of name, address, email,
but common sense for the future
might be wait until we meet them halfway,
before bringing them home.

Careless Consumption

The tide slowly ebbs
from Florida shores
so tourists walk the beaches
without getting wet,
never wondering
why there are no more seashells.
The ocean looks the same to them,
not realizing the muddy water
was once clear blue,
completely untainted.
The fishes are departing
scooped up in massive nets
that do not recognize
the need to feed tomorrow,
the only concern
money to be made
filling the table, the hungry
only concerned with eating,
far more important
then depleting the Earth.

Dictate

Statistically speaking
most humans
prefer to be told
rather than asked
to do this or that
at the behest of someone
rarely concerned
with the needs of the people.

Political Reality

Voices raised against Trump,
sensible or stupid,
have one thing in common,
they are all right.
We know what he is.
We knew before he got elected
in a brilliant campaign
worthy of a Mussolini,
not quite as coercive.
So there are calls
questioning his sanity,
intelligence, ability,
moral and mental fitness.
Yet protesters have forgotten
the line of succession
with someone harsher,
someone dumber,
waiting in the wings,
leaving us to wonder
'shall we leap
out of the frying pan?..'

En Attendant Godot

So many wait for opportunity
not knowing how to make things happen,
so many blindly hoping
things will get better.
Yet the harsh truth
is frightening, confusing,
difficult to accept.
There's only room at the top
for a select few.

The Path of Empire

Empires rise. Empires fall.
The march of time
destroys them all.

Rome. London.
Moscow. Washington.
All alike,
ruled by men of power,
excess wealth allowing
military, economic,
political expansion,
conquering territory,
subjugating natives,
crushing resistance,
until decay sets in.

As money gets scarce
armies get smaller, weaker.
Oppressed people rebel,
refusing to accept the yoke
of foreign tyranny,
always preferring
domestic tyranny.

The resolve to subdue
unruly inhabitants
dwindles, seduced by comforts,
masters too jaded
with material pleasures

to pay the price
to maintain empire,
endure draining assaults
from energetic competition.

Finally the will
that enslaved nations
crumbles under the strain
of multiple disasters
and can no longer maintain
forceful dominance
over captive peoples.

Withdrawal begins
until the mighty sway
has contracted,
while former overlords
struggle to regain
tendrils of prosperity.

Changing Climate

Summer has ended.
The brief, warm time
has departed.
Chill begins to settle
across a devastated land
battered by storm, fire,
citizen unrest,
senseless shootings,
erasing the memories
of pleasant weather.

Viva la Diff...

Psychologists assert
that people are the same
everywhere, differences
trivial compared to
prevalent similarities,
accents, beliefs, attributes,
practitioners of crime
preying on the weak, infirm,
elderly, the helpless,
the poor facing the same struggle
food to eat, a place to live,
a future for their children,
while the rich dwell in comfort
regardless of language,
regardless of country,
united in abundance,
united in luxury,
as everyone else struggles
for a basic existence.

Illusory Ideals

Our belief in democracy
is foisted on us
in grade school,
where we're taught catechism
of life, liberty, pursuit…,
but we're too young to understand
it's only meant for the few.
And for a short while
we're allowed to prosper,
at least some of us,
while the rest wallow in squalor
having lost their hope for the future.

Many of us are so deceived
by a sneaky conditioning process
that we think we're free
and our lives will improve
if we elect the right people
to make things good again.

So we listen to their promises
that have nothing to do
with reality,
yet we vote for them,
install them in high office
and when they make things worse
take out our anger on scapegoats,
blame anyone, any group,
rather then accept the bitter truth

the oligarchs will not allow
inconvenience to their comforts,
despite having more then enough
to share with the needy.

Hurricane III

The storm didn't seem that bad,
but I didn't get where I was
by avoiding possible trouble.
I told Earl, our handyman,
to get a bunch of sandbags,
just in case.

When Jennifer went from category 2,
to category three, I told Earl
to put up the storm shutters
on the downstairs windows.
Then I sent him to get gas
for the generator.

I sent Maria to buy water,
and a lot of other things
to make us comfortable,
cause I wasn't evacuating.
I even had Earl put the small powerboat
on a trailer next to the house,
just in case.

The storm changed to category 4
and Darcy got nervous.
"Shouldn't we consider leaving?"
"Hell, no. And go to some ratty school,
sleep on some dirty cots,
next to who knows what?
We're staying here."

I sent Earl home.
He lived in a shack
out there somewhere.
 I sent Maria home.
I don't know where she lived.
But I wished them good luck.

Jennifer was blowing like wild.
The rain was pouring down.
We were high enough off the beach
that our five foot retaining wall
would stop most of the storm surge
and we always had the escape boat,
just in case.

So we settled down
in front of our entertainment center
resigned to endure
until the storm ended.

A House Divided

Once upon a time
love of country
wasn't a crime.
So it may have been
mythological,
since we never were
the land of the free,
except for brief moments
historically.
Now a great peril
endangers the future
of a declining nation
that can no longer afford
the burden of empire,
while an irresponsible leader
threatens nuclear war,
attacks the environment,
shatters the fragile fabric
that barely holds us together,
until we are separated
from the ideal of unity.

Dreamscape

As I get older
my dreams get stranger,
with infrequent nightmares
as my id evolves away
from torments of youth
that required unconscious enactments
to prevent madness.
Most of my dreams fit
the standard definition,
wish fulfillment, problem solving,
but once in a while
a unique dream occurs
that I actually think about
in an effort to understand
the inner workings of my mind,
yet I can't comprehend
how or why I had
a comical farce dream.

Omnivoracious

Some humans study
life on planet earth
to better understand
the nature of things.
In modern times
they make documentaries
of the strange and mysterious.
But nothing is stranger
Then the human race
a peculiar creation
that defies understanding.

There is no doubt
that most people are good,
wanting a better life
for their children.
But two extremes
pervert our aspirations
to improve ourselves.
Criminals who victimize
their fellow beings,
whether domestic violence
or gang related,
usually small casualties
only affecting a few.

The worst offenders,
those who exercise power,
often beyond the law,

devouring the land,
polluting the seas,
poisoning the air,
endangering the future,
their crimes so great
yet they rarely see a tribunal.

There is a common parallel in Nature
where the alphas dominate,
yet many thinking people
cannot imagine this applies
to our species, citing reasons
to differentiate us
from the animal kingdom.

But some conditions apply
if we observe the reality
of the rule of the oligarchs,
who control the mechanisms
that regulate existence,
since we rarely see them
mostly concealed from the public eye,
distracting us with terror, racism,
all the conflicts that isolate us
and prevent useful action.

The tables of the wealthy are plentiful.
They feast while many go hungry.
They have more than enough
to share with the needy,
but that is not their way.
The greed of the privileged
leads the rest of us to disaster,

since they will not prevent
the threats to existence.

Artificial intelligence
may develop fast enough
to take charge of the means of production,
improve the environment
ensure the Earth is habitable,
since the diminutive minds of the 1%
refuse to recognize our peril.

Some foolish mortals fantasize
that benevolent lizards from Tau Ceti
will come to our assistance,
rescue us from destruction
before our atmosphere evaporates.
That is as farfetched as hoping
our kindless masters will see reason
and join with the rest of us
in preserving human existence.

Motive Power

We flock to cities
to escape the perils of nature,
clinging together
to maintain safety,
isolated in a place of strangers,
save those who build community
banding together for security,
wanting to improve conditions
bonding in friendship for comfort,
in a relentless world
full of perils
that may strike any time.

Progress III

The last time I drove
on I95
65 mph,
the slowest car on the road,
I saw lane changes
without warning
at 75 mph,
tailgating at 75 mph,
texting at 75 mph,
metal machines
barely under control
at excessive speeds,
drivers totally unaware
of the constant danger
of death and destruction
making me yearn
for driverless cars.

Cities

All cities are related
with the wealthy few,
struggling middle class
aspiring to something better,
and the burden of the poor,
crushed by the knowledge
that few will escape
the disease of poverty.

In some cities
there is an effort
to assist the needy,
limited of course
since other interests prevail.

In other cities
the poor are cordoned off
as far as possible
from the gardens of prosperity,
hoping they'll go away,
at least not disturb
the well-to-do.

Other cities
train the police
to contain the undesirables,
allowing the use of force
to keep them in their place,
away from their betters.

Harsh cities
use plainclothes and secret police
to control the masses,
forbidding dissent,
ruthlessly smashing
desperate protest.

Electoral By-Product

I worry about our citizens
who voted for our president
and wonder if they approve
efforts to dismantle healthcare
for millions of Americans,
intent to negate treaties
with friends and enemies,
some with nuclear consequences,
assault on environmental protection
already insufficient to slow
the deadly threat of climate change.
The list of ignorant attacks
on the future of our nation,
facilitated by tax cuts
that will benefit the rich
and pauperize the government,
is punctuated by unseemly tweets
from a self-centered opportunist
surrounded by the submissive,
too dumb or greedy
to resist their masters
in a poverty stricken country
bereft of wisdom.

Hurricane IV

Gol darn suma bitch.
Who he think he is?
Telling me this. Telling me that.
'Earl. Get more gas'.
'Earl. Make sure the boat's ready'.
Man. I hope that storm surge
wipe away his fat ass,
his nasty, big mouth wife
like a ugly old turtle.
And those snotty kids.
Well maybe not Miranda.
She be almost thirteen,
just about a woman.
It serve them right if I take her.
So let the others drown.
Me and my brother come here first.
If the ocean don't get them,
maybe we will.

Unawareness

Autumn creeps into the city
on tentative toes
uncertain when
to denude the trees.
Oblivious people
mostly don't notice
the leaves begin to fall
announcing change of season
that will only have an impact
when cold winds begin to blow.

Something is Rotten

A madman goes on a rampage,
kills innocents
and we quickly forget,
except for the bereaved.
A terrorist goes on a killing spree
slaughtering innocents
and we quickly forget,
except for the bereaved.
Our fear of lack of opportunity,
our struggles to earn a livelihood,
our worry for the future of our children
isolates us from the harsh reality
that our rulers do not care
about our well-being,
or they would make changes
to diminish the violence
that complicates
a difficult life.

Tocsin

I understand the 1%
do not care about the rest of us.
But shouldn't they preserve our country,
someplace for their children to grow up?
Unless they've already got an escape plan
after conserving sufficient resources
so life is sustainable,
at least for the privileged.
But they can't go to the moon, or Mars
our science is just not advanced enough
to allow settlement
on unfavorable environments.
So where will they go?
It looks like they're stuck
on planet Earth,
at least for the foreseeable future.
Do they have a secret hideout somewhere?
Are they too dumb to realize
the safest place in the world
is America, at least until recently?
Now if it's just a rich old fogey
who couldn't care less what happens
to any of us after he kicks off,
that makes a sick kind of sense.
It's almost an archetype.
But what if they have kids?
Where do they think they'll be safe?
Are they too dumb to realize
they should invest in the future

of what was once the richest country
in opportunity,
now an arthritic giant
still capable of recuperation,
if the dumb will take action
and rebuild a struggling nation
for rich and poor alike.

Election Day

Americans go to the polls
many of us believing
we are exercising our right
as citizens of a democracy.
some of us recognize
that our system
is neither fair, nor just,
despite the hallowed promises
of the Declaration, the Constitution,
suborned by the oligarchs
who select the candidates
in an illusory process
that only offers poor choices.

National Climate Assessment

Global warming
a much disputed phenomenon
except to serious scientists,
is affecting the United States
more then ever with impacts
on communities, regions,
infrastructure,
sectors of the economy
and is expected to increase.
Coastal flooding is at a record high.
Ocean warming has hurt fisheries.
Carbon dioxide is warming the planet
and a recent government appointee
reassures us it won't harm humans.
Natural disasters are more frequent,
more powerful, more destructive,
yet when the damage is repaired
most of us go about business as usual,
oblivious to the threat
denied by a tweety leader
that will change our way of life.

Sail On...

The ship of state,
a political metaphor
once popular for a while,
reassured liberals
they were part of a crew
working together
for the welfare of the nation,
never realizing
that the Captain and officers
ruled the vessel
at the behest of the owners,
who ordered its existence
for their own profit,
sometimes promoting from the ranks
to instill hope in those who serve them,
yet neglecting millions
who did not matter
to the fondlers of power.

Congestion

Cities in America
mostly grew before the automobile
filled the streets
in ever increasing numbers,
traffic jams
a daily occurrence
with insufficient room
for buses and trucks
to do their business,
crowded by private vehicles
always in a hurry,
getting more and more impatient,
until road rage incidents
are commonplace

Almost Usurpation

The danger of an outsider
grabbing the reins of state
is that he will not know
how to cope with
endless threats, demands,
the constant need
to confront issues
beyond his conception,
easily manipulated
because of inexperience,
ignorance, refusal to learn
to deal with problems,
obligations at home, abroad,
policies by predecessors
easier to denounce
than understand their importance
to the nation,
proposing legislation
that will damage our future
already in jeopardy for many
by the oligarchs unconcerned
with the needs of the people.

Mid-Autumn

The last days
Of warm weather,
everyone eager to go outdoors
in a committed attempt
to grasp the brief rays
of diminishing sunshine,
as daylight shortens,
brings more darkness.

E Volution

The performing arts
are diminishing
as we grey out.
Opera, ballet,
serious theater without singing and dancing,
high culture departing
and truth be known
it's not meant for all.
Few enjoyed The Flight of the Bumblebee
in grade school.
As writing becomes more elective
e poetry mags proliferate,
some read by more than
mothers and girlfriends.
Most mags profess
aesthetic motives,
never realizing
this may be the last chance
to reach readers about issues
before the oligarchs
take control of the internet,
order our reading,
nullify independent choice.

Discord

Outrage has become
a social norm
as self-righteous protestors
rabidly assail the president
since they are entitled
to foam at the mouth,
curse, hurl missiles,
make a mockery
of reasonable dialogue,
totally convinced
they are acting properly,
as they contribute
to the confrontation climate
that encourages rampages
in our schools, churches,
horrifying the nation
that cannot comprehend
lunatic events.

Hurricane V

Dios mio. What do I do?
Where do I go?
I ask Mr. Jason
if I can bring my kids here.
He say: 'this ain't a shelter.
Take them to the nearest school, Maria.
They'll take care of you'.
"Where the school?" I ask.
"How the hell do I know?
Ask your neighbors. Now get going.
I got a lot to do
before the storm gets here."

Reaction

Another rampage shooting.
The media start explaining.
The Governor explains.
The Mayor explains.
The Sheriff explains.
Everybody has something to say,
but we've heard it before
over and over,
as rampage shootings
become commonplace
in a land of madness
and all the shock,
all the sympathy,
causes less response
as we become inured
to episodic slaughter.

The Rule of Wealth

The Founding Fathers
never believed
that all men are created…
equal,
or they would have made sure
there was a way
to protect the rights of everyone,
not just the few,
reminding us democracy is absent
when we are ruled
by the one percent.

Tormented Earth

Dawn creeps out of darkness
reluctant to reveal
 ravages of man
on once pristine shores.
The beach is littered
with plastic, cigarette butts, beer cans,
all proclaiming management
of diminishing sands.
Owners of the earth
wade in turgid water
tainted beyond redemption
with fossil fuel, human by-products.
The birds are disappearing,
habitat and food sources
rudely removed
courtesy of condos,
yet we still swim, surf,
in this polluted ocean
most of us uncaring
for the endangered planet.

One Nation

America,
just when I think
I've seen all you can do
to inflict harm on our citizens
you're full of surprises
and invent more ways
to discomfort our people,
something dreadful occurs,
reminding me
of your capacity
for atrocity.

Brainwashed

Americans believe
that we are free,
live in a democracy,
have inalienable rights,
and cannot conceive
that when money rules
the average citizen
cannot participate
in our intricate system,
since he/she cannot afford
to run for elected office,
unless he/she serves our masters,
and is rewarded,
just like feudal lords
reward loyalty,
more important than honesty
in a captive nation.

A New Age

Terror has become normal
ingrained in people everywhere,
reinforced by the media
thirsting for disaster
to titillate audiences
by relieving suffering
as long as it's someone else's.
If it comes too close
to the vicarious
the thrill is gone.

Trying Times

Frightened citizens
go about their normal days
with increased apprehension
as prices rise,
rents go up,
health care dwindles,
the simplest choice
stopping at the supermarket,
requires decisions.
What to buy?
Increased costs
place items out of reach,
remembered luxuries
eliminated by necessity.

Euronomics

In the shops
the tourists come and go
empowered by the euro
and look down at Americans
once so superior,
now reduced in status
by the fall of the dollar.

Tests

Hurricanes, floods, fires,
ravage the land
killing people,
destroying homes,
businesses,
lost lives and incomes,
further testing a land
already conflicted
with insufficient resources
to meet challenges.

Hurricane VI

I'm glad Daddy said no
when Earl offered to stay
after Maria left the guest house.
He gives me the creeps.
When he's working on the grounds
he looks all the time
at my budding breasts,
at my body in a bikini
when I'm at the pool.
Not like the dorky boys at school
who look when I'm not looking,
but blush when I catch them.
He has this animal look
like he wants to… you know what.
Sometimes when he's near the pool
he puts his hand on his thing,
looking at me all the while.
I'm glad he's going
cause he scares me…
Not like the safe boys at school.
But sometimes I wonder
what it would be like
doing it with someone like him.

Threat Board

I think about the threats
facing my country
domestic and foreign,
hostile powers, competitors
in a world overrun
with weapons of mass destruction,
nuclear, chemical, biological,
sufficient to end a nation,
or the entire planet.
Racial divisions at home
prevents dialogue
as well as the crushing burdens
of poverty, homelessness,
diminishing opportunity.
We're plagued with leaders
elected by a minority
who wish to disassemble
the benefits of the majority.

Suspension

The days get cooler,
the nights colder,
more and more grey days.
Some say climate change.
Others say nay.
It is difficult to tell
what is or is not normal,
allowing many to ignore
the need to reduce
polluting fossil fuels.

Relocation

Many governments
build housing for the poor
often a benefit and curse
at the same time,
since social services
rarely accompany relocation
leaving residents adrift
with insufficient resources
to cope with new conditions.

The Chinese government
has built entire cities
for several millions
uprooting them
for a new way of life
completely unprepared
for a foreign environment
confining them to hi-rises.

Freedom State

Whether alone
in public space,
isolated in a crowd,
or solitary confinement,
we are only prisoners
when we stop thinking
about the issues
of our times.

City Traffic

American cities,
at least on the East Coast,
weren't designed, just evolved.
When the horseless carriage
coursed narrow streets
no one imagined
millions of autos
would jam the avenues
at rush hour,
at least most of the time,
so slow traffic
only inconveniences
the important few
who could not endure
another rush hour.

Armed and Ready

Every time a murderer
goes on a killing spree
with automatic weapons
it should remind us
that profit to the gun industry
is more important then public safety,
and murderous rampages
should never be allowed
to interfere
with the sale of guns.

Democracy in Action

Election Day
in New York City
and the usual candidates
will be elected
in a democratic process
that includes judges
running for office
without opposition
and few voters
even heard of them
who will make judgments
in the law courts
on ignorant citizens.

A Sporting World

Across the globe
wars rage,
natural disasters abound,
tyranny reigns,
yet sports exist
in every country,
coaxing people to forget
all their troubles
as they root for their team.

Primordial Response

Fear of the machine,
accentuated
by the growing loss
of fear of Nature,
except when propelled into panic
by flood, fire, hurricane,
since for urbanites
the natural world
generally seems benevolent.
Our primitive selves
require something to dread
so we select the machines
that abused so many,
replaced so many,
forgetting that men
make the machines,
operate the machines.

Skating

Eager skatersrush to the rink
in Bryant Park,
first getting wrist bands
to prove they belong,
then to the lockers,
or skate rentals,
pushed by the crowd
urgent to get on the ice
for a short escape
from city constriction.

News Reports

The President says:
Russia didn't interfere
with our elections,
so of course it must be true.
The new E.P.A. head
is firing the scientists
who believe in climate change.
More and more men are guilty
of harassing women.
Road rage incidents
end in shootings.
A puppy in a pet shop
is stolen by a couple.
And endless amounts of sports,
all kinds for all tastes.
These tidbits just a hint
of what goes on daily
that we never hear of,
suggesting to some of us
we have no idea
what really goes on
in this complicated world.

Sports Fans

I sometimes feel sorry
for the ancient Roman populi
because they didn't have
major sports teams
and didn't experience
the agonies of defeat
the ecstasies of victory.
Then I remembered
they had bread and circus,
and knew how to root
for favorite contestants.

Unconcern

I sit in the park,
people nearby relaxed
enjoying a sunny day,
unexpected in mid-autumn.
No one seems worried
about terrorist attacks,
momentarily calm
in a vulnerable city.

The Way

As long as I am not a monster,
murderer, evil-doer, criminal,
it does not matter what I was,
only what I will become.
My basic obligation
to myself, loved ones,
is to do less harm, more good
as I strive to be
a better person.

Battleground

In the age old struggle
between good and evil
the city is the war zone,
crime and violence rampant
outdoors, behind closed doors,
infinite varieties of abuse
more creatively spent
inflicting suffering
than in artistic endeavor,
casualties growing daily
more and more devastated
by abominable acts
that defy explanation
for their inhumanity.

Seasonal Identity

There is a certain kind
of democracy
in the city in summer.
So many wear t shirts, jeans,
it's sometimes difficult to detect
socio-economic status.
But when the chill of winter
requires outerwear,
the coats of the poor
identify the disadvantaged.

Comparisons

For a number of years
I had a nightmare
that Kim Jong-Un
would unleash
nuclear weapons,
when the American response
would destroy the world.
Now I look at Donald Trump
undermining the foundations
of an already troubled nation
and malignant Kim
almost seems sane.

Winter in Bryant Park

The music from the skating rink
peals across the crowded paths,
tourists and New Yorkers
investigating the shoplets,
buying different foods
unnecessities,
spending freely,
some enjoying themselves
on a sunny day
problems briefly forgotten.

License to...

Taxis jump the light.
Cars go through the light.
Both do not stop at stop signs
urgent to get ahead
even when there's no rush.
They can't stay in lane,
cut each other off,
tailgate, speed,
text, talk on the phone,
let alone the careless,
the drunk, the demented
making the roads
combat zones,
yet all are opposed
to driverless cars.

Shock Wave

The clamor of the city
is mostly ignored
by locals, tourists
used to urban din
only reminded
in the age of terror
when sudden detonation
shocks the senses,
shatters tranquility,
prompts immediate flight
in search of safety.

Enemies of the State

If our officials
elected or appointed
do not act
in the best interests
of our troubled country,
of our suffering citizens,
whether through stupidity,
ignorance, greed, inertia,
the lust for power,
purposeful evil,
mental illness,
they are not our friends
and we should be aware
of their wrongdoing,
even when we're helpless
to prevent it.

Safe Haven

Shoppers go to the mall
many for entertainment
as well as acquisition.
Most don't exchange greetings
but are reasonably polite
and don't crowd or jostle
as they transit the offerings.
Then a loud noise resounds.
Everyone scrambles for the exits
stampeding for safety,
crashing into others
in the panic to escape,
not knowing the cause
but quickly reacting
to the threat of terror.

Democracy on Ice

Skaters go round and round
at the Bryant Park rink,
all ages, sizes, races,
united briefly
with no need for conflict,
the pleasure of skating
erasing differences.

Military Affairs

The Navy is too broke
to buy new ships,
hire new personnel,
prevent collisions.
The Air Force is too broke
to buy new bombers,
maintain old fighters,
retain quality personnel
who don't want to fly drones.
The Army is too broke
to buy new tanks,
bigger artillery
that requires Navy
or Air Force transport.
Then there are the Marines
who the Navy can't afford
to give what they need
to land on hostile shores,
instead assigning them F35's,
the joint strike fighter
another military boondoggle
democratic designers claim
will fulfill the needs
of all services.
Now many of the deciders
have gone to college,
or military trade schools,
making us wonder
if they are as irrational

as they seem
in the way they provide
for our armed services

Pleasant Weather

A sunny November day
in midtown Manhattan,
shoppers eager to acquire treasure,
tourists videoing with their phones,
locals enjoying the lunch time break.
Even the tired old man
wearing the sandwich board sign
for 'The Gents' barber shop
doesn't look unhappy.
The delivery men are urgent,
their bosses don't care
if it's nice out.
Stuff gotta get there.
Most everyone else looks relaxed
a nice sight
in a stressful city.

Break Time

Lunch time in the city.
The hordes of workers
urgent for release
pour out of the buildings,
destinations determined
by income level,
nice meal, fast food, pizza,
but they're all out
at the same time,
illusions of equality
quickly forgotten
when they return to work
and the haughty supervisor.

Preoccupation

I spend time each day
considering the problems,
foreign and domestic
that plague our nation.
I've begun to notice
since the advent of Trump
domestic concerns
take more and more time.